Through my memoirs, first my goal was to know myself and how I came to be; second was to share what I have come to know about myself and the world I inhabit.

My novels were a way for me to live in a place meant for me to die; to create a world of love & respect, using the creative art form to illustrate the best of me and a life of Peace. Power. & Position.

Presently, I offer to you what I have come to learn about the personal sacrifice necessary in order to write with sincerity.

Be Bold. Be Beautiful. Be Blessed.

Peter Mack
#LiveRichDieReady
#PeterMackPresents

"Write Your Bestselling Book in 7 Easy Steps by Peter Mack is a must-have for aspiring writers looking to have their literary work published or simply wanting to understand the writing and publishing process fully. Mack has carefully laid out all of the necessary steps to obtain the goal of becoming a published author; there are a lot of books on the market about this exact topic, but what I found unique with Write Your Bestselling Book in 7 Easy Steps, is that not only did Peter Mack tell you what to do, he explained the how, but most importantly the WHY, and instead of just giving tips he used himself in how all of these tips were effective and crucial to your literary success. He also shared advice he acquired over his twenty-year career – a quick and easy-to-follow read for writers wanting to turn their dreams into published realities."

-Kisha Green, Founder, Write Vibe Magazine,
Literary Consultant and Coach

***

"Part memoir, part window into the creative process of a gifted writer. Peter Mack shows the inner works of the literary world from someone who's been inside and knows the players and the process."
-James Wilson, Co-Author, What The Streets Didn't Tell You

***

"I reviewed Peter Mack's first novel, A Neighborly Affair. We were with the same publisher. I knew he would have legions of fans. His talent was unique. As an author I'm still learning and this book taught me something new."
-Paul Johnson, Author, A Lovely Murder Down South

***

"Graduate level instruction gleaned and shared from decades of hands-on experience. Precise and engaging ... Advanced ... Knowledgeable ... Insightful…"
- Kirkus Reviews

WRITE YOUR BESTSELLING

BOOK

In

7 Easy Steps

Peter Mack

PEN AMERICA BOOK PRIZE WINNER

Dedication

For aspiring writers

With something to say

CONTENTS

Dedication

Introduction

STEP ONE: Outline

STEP TWO: Pacing

STEP THREE: Narrative Tense

STEP FOUR: Character Development

STEP FIVE: Plot Construction

STEP SIX: Scene Arrangement

STEP SEVEN: Ending

PUBLISHING

OUTRO

AUTHOR MEMOIRS & NOVELS

AUTHOR PORTRAIT AND BIO

INTRODUCTION

My writing career began in 2003 after an arrest for trafficking narcotics. For the first time my criminal activities had forcefully affected someone very close to me: my wife. She'd been forced to retire early from her position with the Los Angeles County Sheriff Department.

My shame had doubled when the arresting officer gleefully announced, as he escorted me in handcuffs, that he knew me better than I knew myself. He'd been investigating me for some time, including listening to my phone calls.

The arrest forced me to my knees in prayer. I asked God for mercy. For forgiveness. To please replace my criminal ways with something more honorable than selling drugs. Something to erase my shame. A reward better than what my criminal activities provided.

For the next seven months, after this prayer, locked in a jail cell with nothing but pen and paper for 24 hours a day, I dreamed. At all hours of the night and early mornings I'd awaken to record these vivid dreams in print. The eventual sum of these dreams would become my first novel, *HoodSweet,* published by Seaburn Group/Enaz Publications in 2005.

My dreams were about a young man, after the sudden death of his father, who inherits a drug empire. His struggle is escaping the dope game alive to pursue legitimate business interests while also pursuing love between two women, one who feels perfect, the other who is perfect.

The publishing world can be as equally crafty and crooked as the dope game. I never received one royalty payment for *HoodSweet*. And because I was locked into an exclusive 5 year contract, if I wanted to write another novel I would have to change my name. Thus, Peter Mack was born.

My great-grandfather, Peter Mack, was born in 1889. He was an entrepreneur and family man. Learning more about this great man and the respect he garnered I was proud to write in his name, making it my own.

My first novel as Peter Mack would expand on the theme of entrepreneurship and love. *A Neighborly Affair*, about a wife who is sexually unsatisfied, but before departing a rich lifestyle for her neighbor, must first get her own money, would be published by TRU Life Publishing in 2009.

My prayer had been answered. My writing talent had attracted the attention of Teri Woods, famous author of *True To The Game*. She was one of the most recognizable names in the growing genre of Urban Fiction. She was avidly pursuing authors and buying their manuscripts for publishing with her name on the cover. She'd offered to buy both *HoodSweet* and *A Neighborly Affair* for a minimum of 15k each. I probably would have accepted her offer for *HoodSweet* had I not already signed with Seaburn. But for my first Peter Mack novel, *A Neighborly Affair*, my name was worth more than she offered. I had plans for Peter Mack, and my debut novel would be the start of it all.

There's a famous story about Spike Lee's advice to Matty Rich, who struck gold with his film, Straight Outta Brooklyn. Spike Lee advised Matty Rich to learn the craft of filmmaking. Matty had obvious talent, but learning the craft ensures more gold hits and longevity. We haven't heard from Matty Rich since that one film in the 90s. He didn't take Spike Lee's advice to learn the craft.

Teri Woods said to me on one occasion, "Everyone has one good book in them." I believe this to be true, especially if a writer fails to learn the craft of writing. What I would add is that no one can teach you how to write, but you can learn to be better, even great, if you learn the craft. This is what I'm going to do for you. Share my knowledge of the craft of writing.

With my talent validated by early publishing contracts I sought to learn the craft of writing. I'd always been an avid reader, but now I read for analysis and breakdown of the art form. My Literary & Humanities studies included, but were not limited to masters such as, James Joyce, Fyodor Dostoyevsky, J.A. Rogers, Ralph Ellison, Charles Dickens, James Baldwin, Richard Wright, Matt Johnson and Victor Lavalle.

The study of these masters of the literary art form has been instrumental in influencing my own expression over a 20 year career and 30 published books expanded over multiple genres, including memoir, detective mystery, biography, family drama, romance, erotica, and crime fiction.

Here's a hard truth: Writing is more than telling a story. I will share with you my methods employed over the years that have allowed me to write over 30 books in various genres. I'll share with you my physical, mental and spiritual disciplines that have enabled a deeper level of access to the essence of my stories and voices of my characters.

Writing that resonates should convey a sense of purpose; an introduction and exposé of a larger conversation of social, economic, cultural, or racial import. As a writer it is our duty to transcribe and leave for others a representation of what we have come to know that may be of benefit to others.

Perhaps the 7 steps I share with you will be of some benefit and your next book will be a bestseller. Thank you for allowing me to share these teachings with you.

Peace & Blessings,

Peter Mack

STEP ONE:

Outline

I've been fortunate throughout my writing career to have been embraced by so many great writers in the literary community. Of course there are tricky players in the game, but they tend to fall by the wayside; and exposure to these tricksters, who may cost you money, are worth the price of the lesson. Good people stick like glue, and the reward is that you get to watch each other progress, while assisting one another from time to time.

Teresa B. Howell, a faith-based author, whom I'd approached for an interview and ad placement in her on-line magazine, reminded me that we'd met nearly ten years earlier on Instagram. She was a budding author then, and apparently I'd given her great advice and motivation to begin her writing career. This was a boon to my spirit. I was very happy that she'd not only written several books, but was expanding her reach and brand as a literary and publishing professional.

Creating an outline is the bedrock to a great book. This is the one, most important advice I offer to aspiring authors. And keep writing, is another solid piece of advice. The outline is the skeleton for which you clothe with words of muscle, tendons and ligaments; for which you place the heart and vital organs that give it life. The creative art is in clothing the skeletal outline.

The most effective outline which works best for me is the one that supports the rubric of a beginning, middle and end. In other words, an act of three parts. This rubric allows the writer to create an outline which makes easy the transition from sentence to sentence within a paragraph; and paragraph to paragraph within a chapter; and from chapter to chapter, making up each part of a three act play or book. Beginning. Middle. End.

The outline not only allows for a cohesive transition, moving the narrative along, it allows the writer to effectively arrange and plot the book according to character, situation, resolution and time of day. This rubric especially works well if you have multiple main characters and subplots.

If not for an outline I would never have been able to write my debut Peter Mack novel, *A Neighborly Affair.* Because of the multiple characters, subplots and individual narratives that are interwoven into a common theme, the novel required an outline capable of keeping all the moving parts in place as I connected the dots.

Below is an example of an outline for three chapters. Within each chapter you have a beginning, middle and end. This three part arc represents the introduction of a character, action or resolution.

Chapter One

- begin

- middle

- end

Chapter Two

- begin

- middle

- end

Chapter Three

- begin

- middle

- end

For example: In the first chapter the outline could represent the three parts of a day or the introduction of three separate characters. It could also represent actions or a combination of all the above. As a writer this is where your creativity is harnessed and expressed.

An effective outline that fully expresses a beginning, middle and end is written for triplicate exponential; meaning divisible by three, usually 27, 36, or 45 chapters, depending upon length of chapters, which we'll discuss more about later in STEP TWO: PACING.

For subplots the outline allows the writer to explore and manage these within the beginning, middle and end of chapters.

When creating the outline this is where you decide what, when, where and why a person enters or something happens. The beginning, middle and end within each chapter are guideposts to move the action along, keeping in mind the arc of the narrative, subplots and main plot.

If a subplot is introduced within the first 3 chapters, it should be resolved by chapter 18 of a 27 chapter book while advancing the main plot. As a writer feel free to introduce your plots and characters as you wish, and resolve them as you see fit. The outline is only a guide. The creative process will often veer away from the outline. This is fine. This is art. What you'll find is that the outline is instrumental in organizing your thoughts while you place the muscle, heart and lungs on the body to give it life. To the extent you do this well is to the extent you veer from the outline.

- **Beginning** – Bond with the reader. This is the moment to tell the story that engages the reader with curiosity, shock or surprise. The beginning is expressed in the first chapter, chapters 1 – 3, or 1 – 9, depending upon the complexity of main plot or number of subplots.

- **Middle** – Become intimate with the reader. This is the point when the writer connects details to the topics. Here the reader is given context and peek to the possibilities of resolution or twist in the narrative. The middle can be introduced during chapter one, the whole of chapter 2, or chapters 4 – 6, or 9 – 18, depending upon number of subplots or complexity of main plot.

- **End** – Conclude with full circle of facts. This is the moment when the resolution of the main plot is supported by the subplots. Readers are offered a peek into the end during the middle chapters, but not until the ending chapters is the resolution revealed.

This may sound confusing, but trust me, once you create your outline of open bullet points and place your characters, action and verbal notes in the chapters as beginning, middle and end to move the action along, you'll see it coming to life.

Your outline doesn't have to be as multilayered as mine. But it is important to lay out your proposed book in a similar format which allows you to chart the action character by character, scene by scene, and chapter by chapter until all three acts of your book are complete to its end.

One final note: Don't be surprised or concerned when your last nine chapters begin to veer from your outline. This is the creative process. By this time the characters and action have determined a more cohesive and dynamic outcome. This happens to me all the time.

STEP TWO:

Pacing

People, aspiring authors, often ask me for advice about the writing process. As I've mentioned before, I suggest that beginning with an outline is of the utmost importance. An outline not only allows you to see the action on the page, characters and scenes take form, but also set the pace of your book.

One such aspiring author ignored this advice, saying that he would simply write as he saw the story in his mind. Well, two months later and one hundred fifty pages he asked my opinion, complaining that he had yet to get to the major conflict of the lead character. I warned him that after one hundred fifty pages it's much too late to begin the action. Had he prepared an

33

outline this mistake would have been avoided and the pacing properly developed.

K'wan Foye, author of many popular novels and publisher, invited me to submit my novel, *AFFILIATED*, for publishing consideration. This novel had been accepted for a contract by Triple Crown Publishing, however I was warned against accepting this contract because of dubious business practices at Triple Crown Publishing.

AFFILIATED was originally written for Teri Woods at the height of the urban fiction book boom. I was prepared to allow Teri Woods to put her name on the series, but had been offered a deal by Triple Crown before Teri Woods could respond. Upon reviewing *AFFILIATED*, K'wan's advice was to pick up the pace at the beginning of the novel. This advice remains invaluable. Create action early, whether it be emotional drama, physical tragedy, or a mental decision for confrontation or otherwise.

Once the skeletal outline is established, pacing is implemented by the length of your sentences, paragraphs and chapters. James Patterson, a bestselling author, provides the signature blueprint for his success, which I've adopted to increase the pace of my novels while keeping the reader engaged.

- **SENTENCE STRUCTURE**

A perfect sentence is descriptive and demonstrates action while offering more detail. A sentence should move the plot forward, evoke emotion or reaction, and reveal motivation. Obviously, this may not all happen in a single sentence, but what makes a perfect sentence is one that makes this all happen in tandem with connected sentences in a paragraph.

"Peter's writing style is unique. Creating eccentric characters is one of his greatest strengths. Expressing imagery through one-liners is another, such as: 'His head feels like a heart with its own beat.' And, 'Starla's sinister giggle sounds like wind chimes on a rainy night.'

-Tumika Cain, Say What?? Book Club

The above review illustrates what Tumika Cain believes are a great pair of sentences from my novel, *LICKS: Dirty. Nasty. Daddy.*

A good sentence:
He walked to the door.

A great sentence:
He quick-stepped to the door in anticipation.

The two above examples represent the difference between a good sentence and a great sentence. The latter offers description, pace and emotion.

• PARAGRAPH STRUCTURE

The perfect paragraph is three to five sentences of composition. This composition moves the pace of the story with easy engagement and attention to detail. Following this 3 – 5 sentence rule will help keep your thoughts concise and to the point without offering details that can, and should, be expressed later.

If your paragraphs run over five sentences with this rule in mind, it's probably for a good reason that benefits the story, so don't fret about this. The good thing about this rule is that it pops the pace and keeps the reader engaged while naturally forcing you to more details further along in the narrative.

A great paragraph also offers details that string previous and future paragraphs together, moving action along while creating curiosity for the future.

This may sound complicated, but don't over think it. The perfect paragraph is accomplished with 3 – 5 great sentences that move the pace, evoke emotion and offer details.

- **CHAPTER STRUCTURE**

The perfect chapter should be no more than five to seven paragraphs before a scene break or the next chapter. The perfect chapter, with 5 – 7 paragraphs will run three to five pages, depending upon the number of scene breaks. If scene breaks number more than three, a chapter may run seven pages with a ten page maximum. This rule allows for a steady pace and keeps the reader engaged.

While your paragraphs string the story together, the chapter alludes to the previous chapter, reminding readers of where they'd left off from in the last chapter. This provides continuity with a simple phrase, thought or narrative direction.

The perfect chapter is the sum of its parts, offering a steady pace which evokes emotion, offers resolution and portends future events. Your chapter should reveal and/or express a full narrative plot, scene or thought while resolving a minor plot twist, emotion or action.

Do not over think this. A great outline will provide the blueprint to accomplish a great chapter. Your creativity as a writer will be enhanced following these steps.

STEP THREE:

Narrative Tense

Narrative tense is not commonly explored as an option to one's writing style. Most writers, myself included, usually take up the common past tense narrative style. i.e., He said; She walked; They laughed; etc.

J.R. Moehringer, Pulitzer prize winning author of, *SUTTON*, introduced me to an altogether new way of writing. Present tense. i.e., He says; She walks; They laugh; etc.

The effect of writing in the present delivers immediate action to the narrative plot and quickens the pace of the story. But there is a risk to writing in the present and it's not accomplished without dedication to the art

41

form. There is a risk of alienating readers and challenging reviewers, as evidenced below in reviews for my novel, *LICKS: Dirty. Nasty. Daddy.*

"It was hard for me to get into the story line."

"I was somewhat lost at times."

"The story was so out there, at times I was confused."

The above reviews reflect readers who were not accustomed to reading in the present tense, nor a novel with several narratives interwoven into the main theme. However, for those who could acclimate to this innovative creative art form were treated to a story that was both engaging and entertaining.

"Good read. Keeps you entertained."

"Urban masterpiece. I couldn't put it down."

"Compelling. Kept me on the edge of my seat."

LICKS: Dirty. Nasty. Daddy. was my first approach using a present tense narrative style. It remains one of my most highly reviewed and best selling novels. Due to the success of this writing style I followed it up with, *AYANA: The Return*, and, *DOMINA: Submission Is A Privilege*. Both feature a present tense narrative along with interwoven story lines.

I introduce this writing style to you so that you may consider the present tense narrative as an option. You'll be challenged to remind yourself to deliver all verbs and adjectives in the present tense. You'll immediately notice that your writing feels crisp and concise.

With any tense that you prefer to use try to avoid beginning your sentences with the same pronoun, especially with extended dialogue.

"He said ..."
"She replied ..."
"He then said ..."
"She responded .."

The above illustration gets boring, especially when it's in the commonly past tense narrative style.

"Take the trash out," he demanded.
"You take it out yourself," she replied.
"I worked all day!"
"So what! I cooked all day."

The above illustration establishes the order of who is talking while allowing the dialogue to increase the pace with less words to be read. You'll also notice a trick to substitute, "said" with another action word that speaks to emotion, "demanded." This transforms good dialogue to great, moving dialogue, even if you use the common past tense narrative.

Now, let's change the above dialogue to the present tense narrative style.

"Take the trash out," he demands.
"You take it out yourself," she replies.

The present tense dialogue evokes a more immediate emotion and slices more cleanly. Below are examples of a familiar narrative. Note the difference in how they read and feel.

PAST: "His head felt like a heart with its own beat."
PRESENT: "His head feels like a heart with its own beat."

PAST: "Starla's sinister giggle sounded like wind chimes on a rainy night."

PRESENT: "Starla's sinister giggle sounds like wind chimes on a rainy night."

As a writer you must remind yourself that you are free to make your own rules. Just make sure your creative expression is consistent and has a purposeful intent. Pushing the boundaries of what's considered normal content or advisable expression is what creative artistry is all about. Be bold. Be innovative. Be creative.

STEP FOUR:

Character Development

Walter Moseley is a master at character development. He follows a simple formula of establishing his main character as someone relatable who has something to lose and fight for. And mostly against complicated odds. At times his characters are sure to be defeated by unimaginable forces, but through sheer luck and determination they are victorious. Everyone loves an underdog fighting for a noble cause. This is someone to root for and feel the pain of loss when it's experienced by a noble character.

Joy Déjá King is also very adept at establishing memorable characters that ring true. She creates an environment in which her female characters are called upon to overcome huge obstacles to obtain an objective. Her formula, as expressed to me when she approached me to write the, *COKE LIKE THE 80s* series, is to write for the audience. This gem was the secret to her success. Sure, you can write for yourself, but this is akin to someone who talks because they like the sound of their own voice. No one is listening. No one is reading.

A great character is someone who is relatable. The reader knows these people in their own lives; as expressed in the following reviews of my novel, *LICKS: Dirty. Nasty. Daddy.*

"By the time I finished reading this book, I found myself comparing people I know to the characters in the book, especially Stash and Noble."

"I could see the characters while I was reading .. Once you start reading it is really hard to put down."

My memoirs and novels are populated with strong personalities that I've encountered in my life. People routinely ask that they be put in one of my books. My response is that it takes a strong personality with distinctive quirks or characteristics. This type of person is easily transferred to the page.

It is the author's job to articulate the character's psychology, motivation, anxieties, desires, etc. This is done through a great sentence. One that conveys emotion, motivation and perhaps frailty.

"I know Buck, Marvin, Brandy, R.L., and so many others that this brilliant author introduced us to."

The above review is for my memoir, *FILTHY: Innocence Lost*, winner of a 2015 PEN America book prize. This sentiment is not unique. Most reviews for this memoir speak to the familiarity of the characters.

This is a testament to being able to transfer the idiosyncrasy of a person to the written word.

* MOTIVATIONAL / EMOTIONAL

Character development includes a pursuit of its motivational and emotional object. Whether the character's motivation be to protect one's children from danger or to achieve finances by way of illegitimate means, the emotional component is expressed though the anxiety, fear, anguish, determination and/or physical risk to oneself. This is displayed through a carefully crafted sentence that evokes the action which is motivational and full of emotion.

* BACK STORY / TRAUMA

A great character that resonates with readers is one that is crafted with history. This history is best not dropped into one place or a single paragraph, which may be tempting. Pacing is key for revealing the entire history of your character. Use the back story and trauma like seasoning to spice up sections of your narrative or parts of a sentence, or descriptive slice of a paragraph. The back story lends motivation and emotional identity to your character. This trauma, if applicable, drives the emotional energy and physical action of the story. These elements should be placed strategically to inform the reader and provide context for the actions of the character, as well as to provide for pacing of the narrative.

* GOAL

Once the character's motivation is established the goal is set. The challenge for the author is to lay out a path that is unexpected in its arrival. With proper pacing, achieved with descriptive sentences, engaging paragraphs and theme resolving chapters the reader is left curious with each successive turn of the page. Do not be afraid to put your initial thoughts on the page, connecting the bullet points of action on your outline. This is where the best creative process occurs. The rewrite is where the loose edges of dialogue and composition are trimmed away or tightened up.

STEP FIVE:

Plot Construction

Teri Woods, author of, *TRUE TO THE GAME*, won wide acclaim with her character driven plot which featured identifiable narratives that resonated with a multitude of readers. She'd offered to buy several of my books, and invited me to write the last third of the *DEADLY REIGNS* trilogy because I was adept at infusing memorable characters into a plot line that required breadth and depth. She once shared with me, saying, "Everyone has one good book in them, talent creates several."

Great plots are engaging and without anticipation. Fellow author, entrepreneur and friend, Kisha Green, offered the following review of my novel, *THE FAMILY SWEETWATER*.

"..hands down outside the box writing. The taboo topics are carefully woven into the storyline and the author's creative way of storytelling does not disappoint."

Executing a great plot that is worthy of a book that's 75k – 90k words is challenging for some aspiring writers. Having a great idea or knowing the main action is only the start. This start does not make for a full book. Subplots are needed to connect the narrative and add dimension. This is usually achieved by exploring character back story, trauma, motivation and personal goals.

- **MEMOIR / BIOGRAPHY**

Writing a personal memoir or biography is told usually in the past tense and has an intact plot that is based on an emotional discovery, trauma or decisive event or action that changes the course of the author's or biographical subject's life.

As a memoirist I've explored various formats of the genre over six memoirs. *WATERMELON SUMMER*, *FILTHY*, and *FILTHY 2*, all teen memoirs, are written in a novel format which spans the course of successive summers, beginning in 1983. They explore my youthful encounters with girls, bullies, and mischief, eventually detailing my life in the streets at a young age. This is a very common approach to writing a memoir, but there are other options.

PRISON: Life. Love. Loss., is a memoir written to detail the course my life took over a twenty year period, year by year. It explores my emotional and mental struggles, and professional development as an author against the backdrop of prison politics, administrative segregation and maintaining meaningful relationships with family and women in my life.

IF I SHOULD DIE TONITE: Notes To Self, a memoir of notes compiled during twenty years of incarceration, is a personal collection of journal entries that serve as a companion to *PRISON*, revealing an in-depth look into my thoughts, motivations, dreams, challenges and relationships.

BRER MACK: Struggle & Reward, is a spiritual memoir which explores my personal disciplines with anecdotes of my experiences to show how I've come to know myself, and the virtues necessary to overcome and achieve an optimum reward through struggle.

The above examples are offered to illustrate the different forms a memoir may take. The challenge when deciding to write your memoir may be in choosing for which time period to explore and what is most important to document. After deciding which time period, incident, or experience to explore it's important to choose the moments that have high emotional or physical content that will move the story forward and serve as a catalyst for the changes of circumstance or trajectory in your life.

- **NOVEL / SINGLE PROTAGONIST**

Writing a novel that has a single protagonist can be challenging. At least for me it is. But it is a breeze once you've laid out the action with an outline. My problem is that I can become bored easily with the process of reaching 75k – 90k words for a full novel comprising of a single protagonist's dilemma.

Writing for a single protagonist is easily accomplished if you follow the rule of "three cubed" when creating your outline. For a 27 chapter outline the three parts (beginning, middle, end) is divided by three. Your first nine chapters are the beginning. And within these first nine chapters you are again creating a beginning, middle and end to the first act or opening arc of your story. This is to be done for the middle (chapters 10 – 18) and end (chapters 19 – 27) as well. Create the 3 part arc of each act or section. This allows you to create specific action of emotion, motion and resolution within each part of your beginning, middle and end.

This divisible rule works just as well if your chapter count is more than an easily divisible number like twenty seven. Even at thirty one, simply expand your chapter parts. But the rule of three divisible works best (i.e. 36, 45, etc.) to easily manipulate the beginning, middle and end acts of your book.

- **NOVEL / MULTIPLE PROTAGONISTS**

Writing a book with multiple narratives that are interwoven into a single plot is my signature flow. This way of writing for me was born from both the challenge of creating a 90k word story involving one protagonist, and the fact that I always have several topics to explore and have been impatient to wait for the next novel to write in order to do so.

A NEIGHBORLY AFFAIR, where I first introduced several main characters whose narratives were interwoven into a single plot, forced me to invent an outline that could categorize and hold several narratives with interwoven arcs that mesh throughout for a common end. This method gets me to 90k words without much effort.

My bestselling novel, *THE FAMILY SWEETWATER,* is another example of interwoven plot lines involving multiple main characters. If you're like me and favor writing books that address several socially relevant issues involving multiple characters I recommend reading and studying my approach in the aforementioned novels.

LICKS: Dirty. Nasty. Daddy., a bestselling novel, is another example of multiple main characters' narratives interwoven into a single plot. *LICKS* contains three novels which introduces new characters and subplots with each successive novel, weaving the trilogy together into an even more cohesive single narrative. *LICKS* is reviewed as an, "Urban Masterpiece", and I must admit that I had great fun exploring the topical subject matter and complex emotions of the characters.

STEP SIX:

Scene Arrangement

Integral to the tone, pacing and engagement of your book is scene arrangement. It is also a strategic way to assist in the layout and chronology of your outline. Characters are introduced in particular scenes not only for emotional impact and timing, but to move the story along.

Cassius 'Ca$h' Alexander, author and publisher, is very effective at creating scenes arranged in a way so as to elicit maximum emotional impact and story projection. This is done by creating scenarios that are both relatable and unpredictable, yet when executed deliver a cathartic experience.

- **TIME LAPSE**

Proper scene arrangement contributes to time lapse and arc of your chapter with a beginning, middle and end. For a chapter, or first three chapters, to create a full arc, each of three scenes can be divided into morning, noon and nightfall. This placement provides a natural advancement of the narrative and creates a beginning, middle and end arc, while allowing for the introduction of new scenes and characters for an interwoven storyline involving several subplots.

- **PAST JUMP CUTS / MEMORY**

Installing past events into a narrative can be an effective way to introduce some element of a back story to a character's story line. This is most conventionally done using italics to denote a memory. A more innovative way, that continues a simultaneous trajectory forward, is to install a memory of past events into a current narrative thought or dialogue.

"Miriam's thoughts went back to the morning men entered her father's house to discuss the debt he owed. She had no idea that this meeting would result in never seeing her beloved homeland again and find herself purchased for marriage in the United States only three years later."

The above passage is an excerpt from my forthcoming novel, *IMPORT*. This is an inventive way to provide both memory and back story to a current situation that begs an inquiry for more details, giving room for more character building later in the story.

Scene arrangement should support the narrative for place and action, moving the story or dialogue for a specific destination or cathartic experience that speaks to the arc of your narrative.

SARAH'S DREAM, a critically acclaimed novel which comprises multiple main characters with interwoven storylines, is an exemplary example of creating scenes which are inhabited by multiple characters and narrates separately in subsequent arcs of the novel from each character's point of view. This style of interwoven narratives, whether narrated within same arc or subsequent arc, is made possible by creating a detailed outline that forms multiple arcs within all three acts of your book.

STEP SEVEN:

Ending

James Patterson, bestselling author, is a master at creating a dramatic ending even if you know that the protagonist must survive or the plot must unfold to a satisfactory conclusion that satisfies the unexpected. However, before getting to the ending there is a wrinkle in the narrative that breeds doubt as to its eventual assumptive conclusion, allowing for an extended episode of struggle before a reward.

A great ending is the culmination of a proper investment of motivation and emotion into the characters and their narrative. Having thus engaged the reader properly the ending must be equally as engaging to allow for a cathartic experience.

"*DOMINA: Submission Is A Privilege*, was indeed enlightening. It paints a picture of a broader view of the BDSM lifestyle. It's layered with funny, interesting characters."

The above review is for my biographical novel, *DOMINA*, read by Georgia Mitchell, author and publisher. *DOMINA* is illustrative of multiple narratives of fiction woven into a biographical account of a working dominatrix from Los Angeles.

This was a fun novel to write, drawing on familiar people from my life, including my grandparents, uncle and Nisha, a special lady friend. The character of Kabooby is real. Genie DuBois, the sexy matronly lady, is also based on a personal friend.

Regina Bolton, of whose Domme lifestyle the novel is based, revealed details of her life over a six-month period of regular phone conversations. She was amazed at how I was able to mine the details of her life and weave them into a biographical novel.

I mention *DOMINA*: *Submission Is A Privilege*, to offer an example as to the importance of crafting an ending that resolves the narratives with equal attention to the arc of their stories. To achieve this your ending, though it represents act 3 of your book, must also have a beginning, middle and end.

- **A note about *DOMINA*.** The paperback version offers a new character with an extended ending. This was done as a creative enterprise to offer readers something more for their paperback purchase and experience.

- **BEGINNING**

Using the divisible by three rules, a twenty-seven chapter book will leave the last nine chapters for act 3. Consequently, the beginning section of act 3 will be chapters 19 – 21. These chapters form a beginning narrative arc that approaches the end while introducing the resolution of subplots as they inform details for the following six chapters which represent the middle and final arcs for the ending.

- **MIDDLE**

The middle arc of the ending can be used to provide a surprise twist to a predictable ending. These three chapters provide a perfect mini-arc to narrate a subplot that bleeds into the final three chapters for a surprise ending.

- **END**

The final three chapters are pivotal to keeping the reader engaged and providing a cathartic experience. The first two chapters of your final arc are best used to resolve the main character's narrative, discovering secrets or accomplishing a goal. The final paragraph is cathartic and a resolve of all character narratives and main plot.

Publishing

Early in my career, fellow author and friend, Kisha Green, shared with me that you never know what sort of situation or publishing arrangement in which authors are engaged. I would learn the truth of this bit of insight in my own writing career. I've had two literary agents who didn't do much in the way of protecting me against fraudulent publishing contracts. When sought after, I was able to secure four publishing contracts with traditional publishers that served to introduce me to new audiences and propel my career. Having published with independent publishers, I've also ghostwritten and sold novels exclusively for which I'll receive no further royalties. I've found satisfaction with self publishing independently, which has allowed me to retain republishing and film rights to 80% of my catalog. In other words, I own my masters, which are invaluable to the fulfillment of my vision of adapting my novels into films.

*TRADITIONAL PUBLISHER

A traditional publisher is an established publishing house that handles all aspects of publishing and marketing a book for an author. A monetary advance is usually offered to an author for the rights to publish your book, which is recouped by the publisher against sales unless otherwise stipulated in the contract. The publisher will provide professional services such as editing, proofreading and cover design. The publisher takes care of printing, warehousing and distribution, including making the book available in book stores and libraries. The publisher arranges for editorial reviews and book signing events, and may use their connections to schedule interviews. The publisher pays the author royalties from sales of the book.

Usually, a traditional publisher requires submission by a literary agent, but not always. If so, the publisher will make this clear in their submission guidelines. The wait time to hear from a traditional publisher is usually 3 – 6 months, or can be as long as 9 – 12 months. Traditional publishers typically pay 10% royalty on sales, but this number can rise to 15% - 20%, depending on the terms of the contract. And royalties aren't paid until any monetary advance is recouped by the publisher.

The potential negatives to a traditional publishing contract are the writer usually has no say in book design, pricing or marketing strategy of the book. And there is the chance of being cheated out of royalty payments by the publisher, if it is a smaller, independent publisher.

*HYBRID PUBLISHER

A hybrid publisher is a publisher that shares the costs of publishing and distribution of the book with an author. In this model, the author pays some or all of the production and editorial costs in exchange for the publisher's expertise and higher royalties. Hybrid publishing combines elements of both traditional and self-publishing, and is a collaborative way to share risk and rewards.

Hybrid publishers have editorial criteria that determine which books and authors they will publish, and they ideally have a vested interest in selling the book. They also offer value that the author might not be able to secure on their own, and are recognized in the industry for their quality. In return, authors receive higher royalties than they would from a traditional publisher, often around 50%.

*VANITY PUBLISHER

Often referred to as a Vanity Press or Subsidy Publisher, this publishing house is where the author pays to have the book published and signs a restrictive contract which involves surrendering significant rights.

Vanity Publisher is not to be confused with hybrid publishing, where the publisher and author collaborate and share costs and risks, or with assisted self-publishing, where the author pays publishing services to assist with self-publishing your own book and retain all rights.

Disadvantages to a vanity press is they sell you on publishing your book for an extremely high fee and also receive royalties from your sales. They then charge high marketing fees with unproven results.

*INDEPENDENT PUBLISHER

Independent publishers are self-employed publishing companies that are not owned by large conglomerates. They are often run by individuals or groups who are passionate about books and publishing, and can have a unique perspective. Independent publishers are more likely to take risks on different material and publish innovative works, and they are not as connected with sales figures or market demands as larger publishers.

Independent publishers can be small, and some are called Micro Publishers. They often specialize in a particular genre or niche market. Some advantages of working with an independent publisher include: More creative license; expedited timelines; more personal attention; and you don't need a huge following to get published. You can give input into the story direction, cover art, and audience.

However, there are some disadvantages to working with an independent publisher, including prestige and industry validation. It can be hard to get into bookstores unless the publisher has secured a distribution arrangement. Also, no literary book prizes unless your book is submitted to an organization which rewards independently published books. Authors have to master a lot of systems and processes which can be an early learning benefit for new authors.

*The BRU CAPO Company

The BRU CAPO Company is a business and media services company dedicated to the success of literary professionals and entrepreneurs.

Authors who wish to self-publish, making their book available on Amazon and other online venues in paperback and eBook, the BRU CAPO Company offers publishing assistance with all aspects of the publishing process.

The BRU CAPO Company offers personalized services and works with a large network of graphic artists, editors, web designers, entertainment & literary magazine publishers, radio hosts, reviewers, and social media marketers to insure exposure and success of authors and entrepreneurs.

The BRU CAPO Company is unique, as a self-publishing assistant, in its ability to bridge the gap to a successful venture by reliable literary professionals with a history of providing quality service and results.

The advantages of working with the BRU CAPO Company for authors is input and control of the final product, including pricing, cover art and marketing. Authors retain full rights and maintain full access to their online sales account and promotion management. Authors receive full royalties from book sales. Unlike any other publishing arrangement elsewhere, the BRU CAPO Company does not receive any portion of book sales. Authors maintain full control of their account.

The BRU CAPO Company is a division of Peter Mack Presents, LLC. Learn more about their services and opportunities provided for authors, literary professionals and entrepreneurs by visiting www.PeterMackPresents.com

Outro

Now that you know how to position yourself to write a bestseller, what is it that you want to say? How relevant and honest are you prepared to be? What would you like the reader to feel after the last page is turned?

In addition to these seven steps, I advise that you add the following books to your library of resource material.

• *ELEMENTS OF STYLE* by William Strunk, Jr.

• *ELEMENTS OF GRAMMAR* by Margaret Shertzer

The physical and mechanical aspects of writing a great book are easy to execute with the proper outline and accompanying steps. However, the hidden gem to crafting a great book is elusive and must be pursued with patience and perseverance. This hidden gem is belief.

Belief has many elements, all spiritually motivated. Belief begins with oneself and the vision you've established. Belief is first established with intention. Stating your intention verbally, through prayer, meditation or affirmation, brings your hidden desire out into the open for the universe to manifest on your behalf.

My personal practice is to begin each morning with prayer, mediation and verbal affirmations with visualization. Envisioning your goals along with verbal cues of identification forms the building model for successfully achieving your goal.

With this daily practice your book outline will take shape and its contents will speak to you throughout the day and while you're asleep. Don't be surprised if your dreams begin to shape and inform your vision. When this happens force yourself to write down your dreams on a conveniently placed notepad or in your app. Don't rely on your memory after you awaken in the morning, you won't have much clarity.

As mentioned at the start my intention was to share with you the tutelage I've benefited from and the techniques I've utilized over twenty years and thirty books to manifest my visions. The difference between those who succeed in achieving their goal and those who don't is execution. Avoid making excuses. Make time in your day to devote to writing at least a page. Once you build your writing muscles with this daily routine, you'll become stronger, soon finding yourself writing ten pages a day without much effort.

I'm often asked how long does it take me to write a book. And people are amazed when my answer is thirty to forty-five days. Understand that after you write your outline, the rest is easy. The story will be swimming in your head every moment you're away from the book, waiting for your return. Dedicating yourself to writing a chapter a day (5 – 10 pages) makes a full novel of twenty-seven or forty-five chapters easy.

Allow me to make a final point. Research. No matter what your topic, it's imperative that you research. For my most popular character, *PRADA*, an intersex woman, who is featured in several novels, including *LICKS*, *AYANA*, and *POWDER*, my research involved reaching out to transgender women and literature to insure she was depicted with respect.

Whether it be time-period, personality types, geography, or whatever, research is paramount to crafting an authentic book.

Lastly, once you've written your book, don't be lazy and neglect the editing process and the rewrite. The details to filling out your first draft is found in the mundane process of reading what you've written. I've often found that if I enjoy reading my own first draft then my readers will especially enjoy my final draft.

Thank you for your purchase. I pray that what I've shared will be of some benefit to you.

Peace & Blessings

Peter Mack

PUBLISHED MEMOIRS & NOVELS

Series

* Stand alone

MEMOIRS (Isiko Cooks)

Watermelon Summer (1983)

FILTHY: Innocence Lost (1984)

FILTHY 2: Dope Boy (1985)

* *PRISON: Life. Love. Loss*

* *BRER MACK: Struggle & Reward*

* *IF I Should Die Tonite: Notes To Self*

* *What The Streets Didn't Tell You*

SIGNATURE MACK NOVELS

* *Sarah's Dream*

* *DOMINA: Submission Is A Privilege*

* *LICKS: Dirty. Nasty. Daddy*

* *COP & BLOW*

SIGNATURE NOVELS (in series)

A Neighborly Affair

The Seduction Of Ayana Cherry: Sequel to A Neighborly Affair

Ayana Cherry & The Tabernacle Glorious

Ayana: The Return

POWDER: The Trial of Ayana Cherry

*

#The Family Sweetwater

Stone de la BRU Familia

S'Murda At Sweetwater Manor

BRENDA: Barely Legal

POWDER: The Trial of Ayana Cherry

*

HoodSweet

So Hood So Rich

Applebottoms & CREAM

The Trap

POWDER: The Trial of Ayana Cherry

*

AFFILIATED: Boss Angeles

AFFILIATED: Ep. 2: Death of A Snitch

AFFILIATED: Ep.3: A Stripper's Revenge

*

Coke Like The 80s

Coke Like The 90s

Note: *POWDER: The Trial of Ayana Cherry,* concludes narratives with characters from multiple previous series' which brings the BRU family together for a final drama filled story of love & hustle.

Peter Mack is the pen name of Isiko Cooks, author of 23 Peter Mack novels and 7 memoirs, including FILTHY: Innocence Lost, winner of a 2015 PEN America book prize.

The prolific author is founder of Peter Mack Signature Apparel and President of The BRU CAPO Company, a business & media services enterprise. He attended Chapman University and is a graduate of the Foundations in the Humanities Program at UC Santa Barbara.

Learn more about this dynamic and versatile author and entrepreneur at www.PeterMackPresents.com

Made in United States
Troutdale, OR
09/02/2024

22496667R00050